A CONFIDENT START IN STAND-UP COMEDY

A beginners guide by James Crawley

Learn how to fearlessly craft material, book your first gig and thrive onstage.

Copyright © 2019 by James Crawley

All rights reserved. This book or any portion thereof may not be reproduced or used in any manner whatsoever without the express written permission of the publisher except for the use of brief quotations in a book review.

www.jamescrawleycomedy.co.uk

Dedication

To my wife, Saskia. For your unwavering support through good gigs, bad gigs and the numerous rewrites of this book. You do an incredible job building your own business, looking after our children and supporting my dreams. I never could have started performing comedy or have written a book on it without you.
Thank you.

Table of Contents

Introduction	4
Chapter One: Finding Your Funny	8
Chapter Two: Crafting Your Comedy	18
Chapter Three: Performing like a Pro	26
Chapter Four: Memorising Your Material	32
Chapter Five: Your First Gigs	33
Chapter Six: Getting Better	37
Chapter Seven: Finding Support	42
Chapter Eight: How To Conduct Yourself	44
Chapter Nine: Go Forth And Comedy	46

Introduction

There is a common misconception that comedy cannot be taught, "you just have to have funny bones" or a naturally sharp wit. This is a complete fallacy.

Comedy has structure and can be taught like anything else.

It may be that some people have either natural, or at least naturally inherited, comic timing. Or a more obvious knack for noticing the funniness in any given situation - but that doesn't mean others can't learn comedy.

Everyone is funny, right?

You don't have any friends of whom you think: "Yeah, Geoff is honest and loyal…but I have never laughed at anything he's said or done."

If you do have a friend like Geoff then maybe it's time to reassess that.

Now, a great (scratch that, the best) place to get started and learn more about comedy in general is by doing stand-up.

Even if you don't want to do stand-up in the long run, I would argue, it's so raw you must be funny. It trains you to be funny. As soon as you step on stage (or that bit of floor dedicated to performers in the pub, café or abattoir you're in) you have separated yourself from the 99.9% of people who will never put themselves out there.

For anyone interested in comedy, stand-up is worth trying. You may hate it (I hear that happens) but you may find something you obsessively fall in love with doing. That's how it happened for me.

Of course, there's a difference between being funny and being a stand-up comedian. There's a process to go through. It takes a lot of courage to set foot on a stand-up stage for the first time.

It certainly took a while before I felt brave enough to give it a go.

I've always loved writing and performing. I studied film studies at uni, and while I didn't find it to open many doors (except cinema doors), I did find people would say: "You're funny. Why don't you do stand-up?".

At the time, I would say: "I'm not sure about the format…" and other unmentionably pretentious things you get away with as an arts student. But I had always loved comedy, particularly stand-up.

A good few years after uni, I began inadvertently dabbling in humour infused public speaking when I was tasked with writing a best man's speech and a speech at my own wedding. I'm not afraid to say, I smashed them both out of the park and got a feel for how great it is to move a whole room to laugh. Suddenly I felt I *had* to try stand-up. Perhaps it's the same compulsion that's brought you to this book.

So in the Spring of 2017, I wrote for 3 months. With the intention of performing in the near future but with no real idea of how I'd go about securing my first gig.

That summer, my wife saw a Facebook post from an old friend who was looking for acts for a new comedy night in a nearby town. She connected us via messenger, and after a friendly introduction I was kindly offered my first slot! (Never underestimate the importance of your existing network when you're just starting out).

I almost forget about that first gig. With no pressure or expectations to fulfil, I tricked myself into feeling calm and collected as I stepped up for the first time. But other early gigs were a different story…

Getting on stage is only half the battle. Really winning over crowds takes confidence and craftsmanship you're unlikely to have at the beginning.

Being a bag of nerves isn't fun. In the first months I'd often find myself really stressing over how things would go. I'd wander around towns before gigs reciting my material to myself over and over and feeling huge pressure to get it right. Or, when on stage, to throw something extra in (material that wasn't very 'me') in an attempt to get an easy laugh.

I wasn't happy with doubting and dissatisfaction which seemed common when starting out. I wanted to learn more to improve as quickly as possible.

I wanted to find out more, not just about what makes people laugh and how to be a more competent performer, but how to book gigs with ease and get known as a good guy on the comedy circuit. So I became even more of a comedy nerd.

I'd soak up all the comedy knowledge I could find. Watching comedians on YouTube, listening to podcasts, meeting up with more experienced comedy connections and watching more and more live comedy.

In turn, I was feeling more assured on stage, being more creative, booking more gigs, and having people come to *me* for advice on how they could have some of what I've got – confidence in comedy. That's not to say I don't have my doubting days too. It's natural.

I did my first workshop on 'How to get started as a stand-up comedian' in Spring 2018. Shortly after, a writer friend suggested I translate all my comedy nerdery into a book.

I said: "I haven't even read a book…" (Because I can't turn it off). But soon realised, maybe I did have some wisdom to impart. And here it is.

This book is not for the master comedian. This is for both the complete newcomer and the beginner-comedian-turned-comedy-nerd like I was.

The comedian or wannabe comedian who's interested in learning the science of successful stand-up even when they're just starting out.

Maybe you've done a few gigs. Maybe you've not done any. Maybe a friend gave you this book and you're thinking: is this really for me?

Well if you want to try stand-up then yes, it is!

Eric Idle once said that comedy is not art, it's science. "You say 'A' while doing 'B' and it's funny".

Everything I learnt through my early years of performing comedy forms the contents of this book.

I like to think I have natural talent (don't we all?) but my secrets to making stand-up work lie in the psychological preparation and 'science' I always keep in mind as a comedian – whether onstage, performing, or offstage, writing.

This book has been written to share my process with you, and help give you a confident start as the comedian you want to be.

Chapter One:

Finding Your Funny

I'm not here to tell you how to be funny. I'm presuming you are funny, at least a little (unlucky Geoff). But the first couple of chapters are designed to help you better understand yourself as a comedian as well as what it is that makes people laugh - so you can recognise the humour in what you're creating and how to craft your material to be as funny as possible.

Recognising comedic style

Let's begin by looking at the many different styles of comedic performance.

You may be familiar with the types of stand-up comedy seen performed both on TV and live. You may shudder at the thought of being pigeonholed. But I find, it's helpful to know your style so you don't get put on a comedy line-up right after an act doing much the same thing as you.

The 11 Types of Comedic Performance Styles

Here are some examples of TV comics and their performance styles. You will find there will be crossover within a comics repartee and they might easily be identified as more than one style but largely they will fit within these categories.

Visit jamescrawleycomedy.co.uk/styles-of-comedy to find examples from each category to help you get a feel for each style. Warning: some of them are rude and sweary and that.

One Liner
Exactly as it sounds, a joke is set up and punchline delivered in one line. Quick fire with intricately structured delivery.

One Liner comics: Milton Jones, Tim Vine, Jimmy Carr, Gary Delaney, Stewart Francis

Storyteller
Again, as it sounds, a story told to hook an audience in, peppered with funniness throughout and a huge laugh at the end. Possibly playing multiple characters within.

Storytelling comics: Eddie Izzard, Billy Connolly, Bill Burr

Surrealist

Talks on something so bizarre it's funny, willing to riff and improvise into the depths of their mind.

Surrealist comics: Ross Noble, Robin Williams, Monty Python

Observational

Noticing things in life and pointing out the humour in them.

Observational comics: Jerry Seinfeld, Michael McIntyre

Physical

More often than not, this may well encroach on surrealist humour. Physical comedy performance borderlines clowning. Humour from movement and action. May include props.

Physical comics: Lee Evans, Spencer Jones

Self-deprecating

Making themselves the butt of the joke but with a dose of good grace.

Self-deprecating comics: Jon Richardson, Jo Brand, Greg Davies

Black/Dark

Comedy extracted from dark or serious places often "going to places you shouldn't". Sometimes comes from destroying one audience member while everyone else laughs at them. Not for the faint of heart.

Black/Dark comics: Frankie Boyle, Ricky Gervais

Character

When a comedian plays a character, or several characters, across a show who is/are constructed for comic effect.

Character-based comics: Steve Coogan, Al Murray

Musical

Plays and sings funny songs or uses inflections of music to punctuate jokes.

Musical comics: Victoria Wood, Bill Bailey, Tim Minchin, Flight of the Conchords

Deadpan

Often a one-liner or storyteller who performs while seldom cracking a smile. Low on energy, high on wit.

Deadpan comics: Jack Dee, Stewart Lee

Topical

Jokes and stories relating to recent events and current affairs.

Topical comics: Adam Hills, Russell Howard

Satirical

Holding up modern society, the government and establishment for ridicule. Can be topical but more pointedly aimed at authority and not restricted to current events.

Satirical comics: Nish Kumar, John Oliver

Alternative/Anti-comedy

So unfunny that it's funny. Plays with conventions and defies expectations.

Alternative comics: Andy Kaufman, Jordan Brookes

Some of these comedy styles are harder to perform at entry level. For example:

Physical comedy may be difficult due to lack of space in small venues.

With Surreal, Character and Alternative comedy it can be hard to get a good reaction if there is no rapport in place with the audience. When we see Steve Coogan we know he's going to play a character, but *you* don't have that luxury when just starting out.

Topical comedy will mean you burn through material quickly, so you only have a limited time to give those jokes a run. I had some great material on the 2018 World Cup but alas, it has been lost to time.

Deciding on your style

Now you've understood the styles of comedy open to you, you can begin to identify what type of comedian you are - or are most likely to become.

For me, discovering my style came pretty naturally. I've always been a storyteller and an observer. I love a good story, and whether I'm meaning to or not I'm often soaking up even the seemingly mundane life experiences around me, and finding the funny in them.

Don't overthink it when you're starting out and it should be straightforward for you too. The easy way to determine the type of comedian you are (or will be) is to ask yourself: what do you want to do? What style of comedy are you excited about performing?

Ideally, and most likely, what you want to do will be what you are good at anyway. Enjoyment translates into an onstage confidence.

If you're a strong joke writer rather than an anecdotalist, you'll likely do one-liners. If you can pick out the humour in everyday life, you'll be a great fit for observational comedy.

There's an open market for all styles of comedy and you shouldn't feel you can't do a certain style based on what acts around you are doing, or the venues around you are booking. At the start of your comedy journey, you have the freedom to experiment with styles and try different things free from audience expectation.

While you should avoid going dark and dirty early on (in my opinion, an opinion shared with numerous comedy competitions) comedy is held in high regard as a bastion of free speech. Most things aren't off limits.

Now, I say most things… I don't have to explain a moral compass to you as to what you absolutely shouldn't joke about, right?

Importantly, you should write so *you* find it funny. Don't write and perform something you aren't comfortable with to give people what you think they will like.

Owning your style

Once you've figured out what works for you, be true to yourself. Be 'on brand' for the type of comedian you are. Don't do a set of light hearted fun stuff and finish with a dark joke about necrophilia. Yes, I did that once. They laughed, but it didn't feel good. (Ok, I did that more than once… Maybe even twice… Let's call it ten. It's tempting to jump on cheap laughs when you're still honing your material!)

Want to make your material as interesting as possible? It's much more interesting if you have opinions on what you're talking about. Giving your opinion gives the audience a clearer understanding of where you're coming from and gives your joke a motivation.

It doesn't mean you have to explain your feelings, or justify your ideas, but through your movements and language you achieve comedy by making it clear how you feel about a topic.

For example, I have a series of jokes about James Bond. I take an anti-Bond stance immediately. Naturally, some people disagree (they love double-o-seven) and the conflicting opinion makes people more interested. Bond lovers and detractors pay more attention but it doesn't impact the audience's reaction to a joke that I don't like Bond - particularly as he's fictional.

Dealing with your worries

It's sad to think that many funny people interested in performing won't take the risk to step on stage. They will let their anxieties hold them back.

In my workshops on getting started in stand-up, I open with a section on "What worries you most about performing?". It's surprising how many of the same anxieties come up and how easily they can be overcome. Here's a look at the most common concerns and how I recommend working past them:

"I'm terrified of public speaking in general..."

Like any performance situation, you'll be nervous when you first start out. This is natural, and even beneficial. Onstage nerves create adrenaline which in turn keeps you highly aware. For one, adrenaline helps open breathing passages in your lungs, which in turn will increase your oxygen intake and help you think clearer.

As you get more experienced, you should find your pre-show nerves reduce. We'll look at tips for a confident performance later - but ultimately, stepping out of your comfort zone and just doing it will be the best step to overcoming any anxieties around being seen and heard by an audience.

"What if I didn't get a reaction? Silence would be the worst!"

If you're concerned that silence is worse than even a negative reaction... yes, it's true, but try not to worry. People attend comedy gigs to react. Usually positively, with laughter. If you do find your material having a negative reaction, this opens up opportunity for you to have a humorous reaction in return. Saving the situation with a joke or bit.

"What if my memory goes blank?"

I think this is a valid concern for all comics, and it does happen even to pro comedians. There's footage of Seinfeld going blank on stage!

I tend to prepare with something in mind I will talk about if I ever do forget my act. I have never had to do this, but that safety net comforts me. (More on this later, I've got a chapter coming up).

"What if I end up going on a tangent?"

Going off on a tangent is the opposite of going blank. But again, try not to worry, some of the best material you will come up with may come out of 'riffing' (making things up on the spot). Don't by any means riff a whole set, but don't feel you can't follow a natural interest when it takes hold of you.

"I'm scared of technical mishaps like microphone feedback..."

The technical quality of your performance is totally not your responsibility. The person running the gig has a duty of care and won't (or shouldn't) let you down!

When technical issues do strike - the best trick is to either comedically acknowledge it or to pretend nothing has happened and carry on. I always try to produce a positive spin from the unexpected. One of my favourite performances to date came about when the microphone stopped working and I had to go micless - there was a new freedom with having both hands and no mic stand in the way.

"I'm worried I'm awkward, boring and unfunny."

Wow, this one comes from a place of real concern. Confidence will come with time and practise and no one is boring or unfunny! Being confident and comfortable is key.

"I don't want to be ignored or not be heard."

This is another logistical problem and wouldn't be your fault. Gigs in thoroughfares and open rooms are often a problem. It means some of the audience aren't there for comedy and as such won't be keen to watch and listen. It's an experience you'll likely go through, but avoid gigs in the main room of a bar unless they have a good reputation.

Chapter Two:
Crafting Your Comedy

Now that you've assessed your anxieties and have a feel for your potential comedy style - it's time to think material. How you approach joke writing will largely depend on the style of comedy that most resonates with you. In this chapter, I'm going to take you through the writing tips that have most helped me:

The 9 Triggers of Laughter

One of the most useful comedy theories I've learnt is the triggers of laughter. Now most comics may not even know or care why people laugh at things they say and do, but there is always a reason. Human laughter is involuntary. And it's been recognised that there are specific causes for human laughter. These can be broken down into the following nine triggers:

1. **Surprise** – The most common cause of laughter in comedy. Every punch(line) is a surprise. Surprise in comedy is where you think a joke is going one way, and then it goes another. The one liner comics mentioned earlier all work with surprise.

2. **Embarrassment** – Hearing someone tell a no holds barred experience of embarrassment is funny. Comedy is about empathy. It makes people root for you, and laugh as well. Or just laugh, if they're a bit mean.

3. **Recognition** – Observational comedy is all based on recognition. I love how when you watch a comic performing observational material, you'll often see audience members tapping their friends going "that's so me/you".

   Recognition based comedy also comes in the form of a 'call back' to your own or someone else's material performed earlier. Russell Howard is a master of the call back, watch his live show and you'll see how much he refers to earlier topics.

4. **Superiority** – Self-deprecation is based on allowing other people to feel superior. Superiority also comes from challenging authority figures. Think Monty Python and how much of their humour was based on jabs at authority figures.

5. **Incongruity** – Yes, the words are getting fancier! This means imposing values on something that shouldn't be that much of a concern. It also features it anthropomorphism (another big word and I spelled it correctly first time!) which is when you put human characteristics on an animal.

6. **Ambivalence** – Quite the opposite of caring more than necessary, ambivalence is not caring about something that you should. For example, being casual about something bad happening.

7. **Release** – When a story goes on and on and on, building up, and when the reveal is shown it causes a huge release. If it's a benign outcome, that's funny. The satisfaction and humour comes from not having to worry any more.

8. **Configurational** – This is where the audience figure out the end of a joke. You leave out the punchline. Sometimes this happens with jokes that do have a punchline and a few people laugh before it's delivered. Configurational comedy is hard to master due to the difficulty in getting everyone tuned in to what you mean.

9. **Tickling** – Let's remember this is the 9 triggers of laughter, not the 9 elements of comedy. You probably aren't allowed to do this in your act but I promised all 9!

Being aware of the 9 triggers of laughter isn't essential to come up with funny material. But I find it useful to know why a particular 'bit' is funny, and which box it ticks to make it a hit with an audience.

These triggers were first identified by psychologist Patricia Keith-Speigel. I was first introduced to them via Jerry Corley's YouTube channel. Corley is an incredible comedian who has been on Letterman, written for Jay Leno on the tonight show, and worked in comedy for over 25 years. He has a brilliant website called standupcomedyclinic.com and responds frequently to questions on twitter with the hashtag #askthejokedoctor.

Putting jokes together

When I teach workshops I don't directly teach on writing jokes. I think joke writing is a personal process which relates to the context of who you are - and I'm not sure I know you...

However, here are my recommendations for how to aid comedy writing based on my personal process. This personal process helps me feel free to experiment and take creative risks that I can later test out on stage:

Keep track of everything

My biggest tip for writing material is to always have a pad with you (or your phone, you hi-tech funkster). Anytime you think of anything funny that could potentially work as a basis for material, write it down.

My notes vary from well-formed longer ideas and stories - such as a story about doing a Harry Potter quiz with my parents (correct, it's a self-deprecating one) - to a single line concept like "cats have canine teeth". With everything jotted down, I can go back and hopefully find something funny in my notes later (spoiler: I didn't with the latter one).

Be intentional with words

There are tricks you can use to make your comedy concepts funnier too. One of them being: be intentional with the words you use. Generally, any word that makes you smile when you say it is funnier than one that doesn't.

One of the reasons that f*** is a funny word is because your mouth naturally produces a grin when you produce a 'ck' sound. Also swearing has shock value – remember that 'surprise' trigger. Dropping an F-bomb can be a bit cheap, and at times you will hear comedians doing a joke that only works if they swear. If a joke doesn't work without swearing, it may be best not to use it. Arguably, at times its necessary for emphasis.

To the same effect, if you need an animal for a punchline then duck is funnier than cow because it makes you smile when you say it.

Structure

There are age-old tropes you may naturally find yourself using as you start out, or you may want to work into your material purposefully. Here's a breakdown of these classic techniques and some examples of how I have used them in my material:

- **The rule of three**

A useful one to know up front, the rule of three isn't solely used in comedy and is regularly heard in speeches – with a list often containing three things "friends, romans countrymen", "blood, sweat and tears" - Nearly every play and film works on a three act structure too.

The rule of three is simply that when you list three things. The first is normal (establishes), the second is also normal (reaffirming the normality) then the third is funny (breaks expectations). For example:

When I started doing comedy a friend of mine said to me: "Your poor kids... I can't think of anything worse than my dad doing comedy!"

I can think of loads of worse jobs for my dad to do: porn-star, pimp, politician for UKIP.

(Notice the nice intonation of each thing listed beginning with "p" as well.)

- **Bait and Switch**

This works on a classic surprise premise. The bait is set with a statement leading towards a logical conclusion. It seems like things are heading in one direction and then switches away to something unexpected. For example:

I recently gave blood for the first time. I don't know if you know, but when you give blood, you get a goody bag including things like a key-ring. Mine says B plus on it, that's my blood type.

My wife said to me: you should be so proud of yourself...that's the best grade you've ever got.

This one works because we understand the premise of a proud partner. But then she launches a zinger at me and it's a self-deprecating surprise, with the longer build-up adding to the suspense. Also, a true story by the way.

- **Pull Back and Reveal**

This is a less used trope and hard to pull off well. It was famously used and sent up in the context of "And then I got off the bus" by Stewart Lee and Richard Herring. The context is more familiar in TV, the idea being a camera shot only shows so much of a scene and then pulls back to reveal more. In terms of stand-up you would use this technique by only revealing so much information, then adding more to surprise the audience at the end.

One of my own 'bits' featuring pull back and reveal is the ending to a long story I tell about discovering a frog in my kitchen and trying to get it to leave – looking like an idiot in the process. Towards the end, I up the ante with: *"At which point my wife comes downstairs to find me in just my pants and a rubber glove, waving at an amphibian"*. The reveal being this added information which I'd previously withheld.

It should be noted that all three of these structural techniques use a surprise laughter trigger and work on the basis of misdirection - with comedy coming from being led one way then suddenly forced another. Misdirection is *so* important. A lot of great comedy comes from misdirection.

Where to start?

If you are really stuck on where to even start writing, challenge yourself to face a completely blank page and think about:

- What do you love?
- What annoys you?
- A problem that you can solve (maybe badly).
- Absurd things in everyday life.
- Slogans of companies or proverbs and sayings that don't make sense to you.
- And of course, stories you love to tell already! Really mine those tales you enjoy telling friends and family. Then mine into them further, because they need to be funny throughout. Get analysing.

Keep it personal

I've already mentioned how important your personal opinions are in comedy but I want to emphasise to you how important it is to own them! Now is the time to take all the stories and witticisms you've previously shared and hold onto them. Comedy thrives on sharing life experiences, now more than ever. Everything you've learned in your life this far can influence and inform your comedy.

Go back through your life, as far back as childhood, and think about the memorable experiences you've had. Good and bad. Is there a way you can pull comedy from them?

Recently Edinburgh comedy awards have tended to be won by shows that really delve into the personal life and/or psyche of the performer.

Plus, look at some of the recent Netflix specials: Neil Brennan: 3 Mics, Hannah Gadsby: Nanette. Personal revelation is captivating.

Chapter Three:
Performing like a Pro

Lots of "facts" are thrown around about comedy performance. One being: you must get a laugh within 30 seconds or you'll lose an audience.

While this isn't *always* going to be the case, it's along the right lines. If you can quickly get an audience to like you, you are most of the way there.

The good news, most people going to watch comedy want to see someone succeed. (With the exception of the odd rowdy crowd who want to see someone fail...) Your audience want to like you.

Here are a couple of things you can do to help increase your likeability factor:

First up, be yourself. You are a beautiful, wonderful, interesting person. And they'll see that (ew, sentiment).

Also, be confident. An audience want to feel comfortable. They want to see someone in charge. In control. If you come across confident you are more likely to give your audience permission to laugh rather than cringe.

Stage presence

If you're not sure how to be confident on stage yet, here are some tips a lot of acts would benefit from hearing early on. These little moves may not seem like a big deal, and may only be picked up on subconsciously, but master these and you can look like you know what you're doing from your very first gig – because you will! Stick with them gig after gig and they'll become instinctive.

Master the microphone

To start with, either take the microphone out with one fluid movement and plant the stand like a flag to one side or behind you. Or, if you want the mic in the stand, stand behind it and lower the stand to be at the right height for you - then hold onto the stand so you don't stray away from it. Being confident with these movements makes you look like a safe pair of hands (no pun intended).

Where you hold the microphone is also key. Hold the microphone so it doesn't obscure your face. Many acts lose one of their best tools (their mouth) by covering it up.

Lock your arm in position and hold the microphone by the handle, not by the head. You are not a rapper (except if you are a comedy rapper... Then, fill your boots).

I also personally prefer it when an act doesn't lean on the mic stand, it's distracting. I've seen some phenomenally good comedians play around with the microphone stand and detract from their act. Don't do it. At the very least because you may screw it up for the next act.

Avoid the nervous wander

With the mic in place, stand still and in the light/middle of the stage. You will see a lot of acts roaming the stage as they perform. Wandering about the stage without a purpose is distracting. If you are to move, have a reason behind it.

On bigger stages (think theatre/stadium venues on TV) moving about can be assertive as there is a lot of space to be used. But on a small stage (or in the no stage performance spot you'll likely start with) there is no need to stroll about.

Deliver to the audience

Look out across the audience. Deliver jokes out and up, not down at your feet. A lot of good punchlines suffer from being delivered to the floor, which suggests a lack of confidence in a joke.

Preparing psychologically

When I was about six months into doing comedy, I met a sports psychologist, Dan Abrahams, at an improv workshop (a little more on improvised comedy later). Dan works as a sport psychologist for both an English Premier League football team and several world-class sports professionals. He's a man who knows his stuff when it comes to performance techniques. Although comedy is not a sport, performance is performance, and several of the psychological tricks he implies have been pivotal to boosting my confidence on stage.

Here's how you can apply them as you start out:

Get your body ready

Get adrenaline flowing and build confidence by adopting a power stance for two minutes before you perform. This will increase your sense of confidence and be reflected in your onstage presence.

To adopt the power stance: place your hands on your hips with feet shoulder width apart. Think superhero.

Before most gigs, I do this and can feel the benefits. Take it, use it, or don't. But it's not going to do you any harm.

Remember your PEACH

Dan also shared his 'Game Face' technique. The creation of an acronym to embody the type of performance you want to give. He has professional footballers using this to enhance performance. I particularly enjoyed hearing about one specific footballer's acronym - and while I can't remember it word for word - I know it included Fearless and Ronaldo. It's working for him, he plays in the Premier League!

I started using my own acronym (PEACH) that may help you and you are welcome to use. Or you could make up your own - what fun.

P – Presence
From early on people picked up on my stage presence being strong. I just carry out the tips already discussed in the Stage Presence section. It works for me.

E – Energy
Going on with energy doesn't mean running on and jumping about, or getting everybody cheering. This is about judging the right energy for the room you're in. Some rooms will like it a little calmer, don't insist otherwise.

A – Attentive
What's been going on in the night so far? Any in-jokes? Any names you can use to make a bit funnier? Did they like a joke earlier that was dark? No? Don't do your dark joke. Be attentive, notice what this crowd likes and personalise for them if you can.

C – Comfortable
Be comfortable on stage. This isn't that different from presence, but you can have presence and be uncomfortable. It can really break the goodwill in the room if you aren't comfortable doing what you're doing.

H – Hilarious
Just be funny! If you get the other one's right, this should come naturally.

When I go through these I embody the action that comes with them before I go on stage. While on stage, I then find these become natural. The more I use this technique, the more powerful it becomes.

When I think Presence, I stand tall. Energy, I start moving my legs and arms, and so on. You have to get yourself in that mode not just think it.

It's also found it useful to remember (thanks again Dan): once on stage, even if my performance drops to a 3/10, I'll try to keep my mindset at 10/10. I won't be put off by one joke that doesn't land.

Now, this isn't exactly Game Face as he teaches it. But it's how I've understood it and applied it to comedy. If you're interested in taking more sports psychology and corrupting it into comedy tools, you can find Dan Abrahams books at danabrahams.com

Chapter Four:
Memorising Your Material

This chapter will help with dealing with the worry of how to remember your material. Even well-established acts write notes on their hand to help with this, and I don't think an audience minds, but I was introduced to a memory technique worth sharing if you want to avoid glancing at the back of your hand.

Another friend (I know, two friends!) and memory expert, Michael Tipper, is a public speaker and trainer in learning techniques. As such he must learn hour long speeches/presentations frequently and practices a memory technique easily transferable to use in stand-up.

Memory is visual. We remember in pictures, not words. So when you arrive at a venue, you need pre-planned image cues to set up around the room. This means, when you look at a certain position in the room during your act, you'll remember a key piece of information to trigger your 'bit'. This is called The Journey technique or the Loci technique.

For example:

As a few of my imaginary visual prompts, I have used a Monopoly board, Harry Potter and a potato.

No matter what the venue, I have imagined a giant Monopoly board embedded in a table on the left, Harry Potter standing on a table slightly to the right of that and a giant potato further along.

This has allowed me to deliver to the audience but still have my visual triggers to help remember a planned set.

More information on this and other memory techniques can be found at michaeltipper.com

Chapter Five:
Your First Gigs

Early on, the be all and end all of Stand-Up Comedy is stage time. Stage time being the amount of performance time in front of an audience you've clocked up in your comedy career so far. This isn't exclusive to stand-up, it's the same for any type of performance based art. On the open circuit (which is to say gigs that feature amateurs, semi-pros and pro's who are likely not on tv yet), people are obsessed with getting stage time. There are tales of big name comedy stars driving for hours to do five minutes to help hone their craft in their early days.

Now, while stage time is important to stand-up success, I believe theoretical learning has real value too. Work on your craft off-stage as well as on. More stage time doesn't *always* equate to more laughs if you aren't adjusting what you do between gigs. Improvement comes from reflection on your performance, not just continually performing the same thing in the same way.

Getting on gigs

So, logistically how does one get on gigs?

Well pre-Facebook I have next to no idea. Post-Facebook, you're in luck, even as a newbie.

The best bit is, thanks to Facebook you can get gigs easily without ever having connected with a stand-up comedian or promoter before! Look at how things started for me: I booked my first gig when my wife happened to spot an old friend post about launching a new comedy night nearby.

And if things don't happen to work out so serendipitously, you can easily be proactive. It's straightforward to find a relevant comedy forum, see bookers looking for acts for their nights, and get in touch.

These forums (aka Facebook groups) are called appropriate, if not clever, names like: Facebook Comedy Forum, The Comedy Collective and more regional specific ones as well, such as South West Comedy Circuit.

In these Facebook forums, you'll find promoters. These promoters are likely booking comedy *and* working a job, dealing with their own life etc… When they put out a call to see which acts would be interested in doing a slot, they're looking for more input than a quick "Me!" or "I'd love to" comment on their Facebook post. Send a proper message or email and have a video ready for those promoters who've yet to see you. Make their life easy. Be professional, be prompt and give them all the info they'll need, otherwise you will not get booked.

As a promoter myself, I have a pretty strict no-video, no-booking policy which helps me cut down on the number of applications I have to consider. The only way you'll get by this is if we've worked together before and I know you have an appropriate style for my night. Which goes on to remind me, make sure your video showcases an appropriate style for the gig you're applying to. Don't apply for a clean night using a video of a swear-filled 5 set.

Types of gigs to choose from

Open Mic Nights can be a good choice when you're starting out, so keep a lookout in the groups for details of these. Some nights have a sign-up on the night policy, others require you to get in touch (drop them a message via their Facebook page).

Then there are "New Material & New Act" nights, great for those starting out to get in front of a warm audience ready to see some new comedy. These are part of the aforementioned "open circuit" - ie, accessible for amateurs and semi-pros alike as well as pro acts trying stuff out.

As you start to get recognised on the open circuit, you can be booked for "open spots" on bigger nights, alongside bigger acts. They may still be unpaid, but this is a step in the right direction - allowing you to get some more established nights on your comedy CV.

As you find your confidence and start attracting attention, you will then be ready to apply for paid middles (the middle spot on a line-up) and maybe opening spots (going on first) if it suits your style.

Eventually closing rooms/headlining (going on last) will be possible for you. In my experience, how long it takes to get to this point is less dependant on the hours of stage time you've knocked up, but your ability to demonstrate your confidence, material quality and stage presence. Videos and great reviews are key to this. Competition wins and, more so, TV credits will fast-track an act there even sooner.

Starting your own night

Once you are comfortable on stage and enjoying gigging, I then recommend starting your own local night. This quickly enables you to establish yourself, while allowing the opportunity for frequent stage time as a host.

I started running a comedy night 4 months into my stand-up career. Not only did it open up regular stage time, but it forced me to: write new material, master crowd work and learn how to network with comics.

I've also learnt just how much work goes into putting on and promoting a night. (Spoiler: it's a lot!) But well worth doing if you want to get better at stand-up.

Don't be fooled into thinking you need to be a pro comic to set up your own night either. When I started my monthly night, I hadn't yet made any significant money from comedy. But I was passionate about sharing great talent and wanted to make a regular slot for myself to perform at a night which had the right vibe for my comedy too. Starting your own night (if you run it effectively, book great acts and focus on building positive relationship) is a quick way to boost your reputation as an act too.

Performing as an MC (master of ceremonies aka. the person who introduces acts and keeps the crowd happy in-between) opens up another opportunity to book gigs too.

MCing will only work for you if your style suits, or you can adapt your comedic performance accordingly. Hosting a gig requires a likeable, high energy performance. I have seen people host gigs differently, but personally I think it works best in this style and opens you up for more booking opportunities.

Other good places to accrue stage time include charity nights, variety nights and non-comedy specific open mics. Although charity gigs and mixed art performances are often less than ideal for doing comedy. The audience aren't always ready for comedic performance following an emotional fundraising talk or an Irish jig, but they may be a nice place to bring some of your trademark mirth and gain fans.

I remember how hard it was to lift a charity crowd after they'd just heard heartfelt talks on debilitating illnesses, but those gigs make you a better comic.

Chapter Six:
Getting Better

How will you progress in comedy? It's a good question and one I think needs more creativity than many afford. Here are my tips for improving aside from doing as many gigs as possible:

Try comedy competitions

Gigging will get you good. Doing competitions will get you noticed. They will also get you performing in a higher pressure environment.

Lots of newcomer contests exist: BBC Newcomer, So You Think You're Funny?, Laughing Horse, Amused Moose and festival specific ones. But competitive comedy is a weird thing, because comedy is not a contest. All acts contribute to a night, not just one. And of course comedy is notoriously subjective.

This is however the voice of a regular comedy competition loser speaking... People who win competitions, or reach the finals, tend to move up the pecking orders at speed.

Competitions: do them and you may feel awful after. But a gig is a gig, and there will be a good crowd at competition gigs.

There are also competitive gong shows. In these, comics have to perform five minutes (sometimes more/less) without being "gonged off" - where the audience vote for you to stop. You could easily thrive in comedy without ever doing a gong show. They do put you in a pressurised environment which puts some people off entirely.

Again worth doing to get noticed by promoters if you are comfortable with that pressure.

Be your own critic

Try to take film or audio recordings each time you gig. You can then review this, and if a 'bit' continually doesn't get the response you're looking for (laughter) then drop it. Don't be too precious about dropping material from your set. It could be you rework it into a different angle or perform it differently at later date. For example, with added physicality.

There will be occasions where you also need to realistically ask yourself: "Am I good enough to do this gig yet?". Be ready for rejection and prepared to never hear anything back from a promoter about a gig you've applied for.

Too many people apply for gigs for a promoter to respond to everyone. Try not to take it personally.

Don't be deterred

Although it's healthy to critique yourself, try not to be too hard. You *will* have gigs that go badly. And it will more than likely not be your fault! Assess what you did wrong by all means, but don't be disheartened. See your failings as learning opportunities.

Securing gigs and impressing audiences is hard to do and keep persevering with. I say this as a straight white man who is about 30 (which most comedians you meet will be). I can't imagine how hard it must be to do comedy from a position of diversity.

To really thrive you'll need a good support network who can pick you up when you're feeling down about your progress and performances too. It's beneficial to have a mix of comedy and non-comedy peers you can call on to both give you honest feedback, share what they're going through – or remind you that you are not solely a comedian but a fully rounded person with value on and off stage. More on finding support in the next chapter.

Know the difference in culture for your area

I live and thus predominantly perform in the South West of the UK. I can't directly advise you on your area – but it's important to realise there is a difference in comedy culture across the country.

London's comedy culture is distinctly different from the South West. In Bristol and surrounding areas, as soon as you have twenty minutes of material and the confidence to pull it off you'll get spots doing it. In London it's five tight minutes as the standard when you're starting out. Many places offer five minute slots but not much more.

London's scene also has a big emphasis on those aforementioned competitions.

In some areas you'll find an emphasis on "you'll need to have done 200 gigs to even apply for this gig", these kind of numbers are arbitrary as far as I'm concerned. Whereas there is credence to stage time being a huge part of improving, one person may take 20 gigs to learn what someone else takes 100 to learn. The trick is to make sure you reflect on every performance to improve. If you're good enough you're good enough. Just make sure you have video or references to back it up.

A bit of comedy folklore - Jack Whitehall did five gigs and got offered a TV show. No source on that but I hear it regularly… I believe it was when he was runner up in a competition in front of the right judges.

Be a comedy nerd

Do workshops and read books (smiley face emoji). I used to think comedy couldn't be taught, but it's now clear to me it can.

Workshops can give you more depth of understanding as a comedian, helping you become aware of new techniques to experiment with and allowing you a safe space to test material, ask questions and get feedback.

There are all sorts of workshops out there. If you tell stories, there are specific workshops for that style. Need help joke writing? Absolutely. Physical comedy? *ding dong* That's 'yes' in physical comedy speak.

Podcasts are one of the best ways to hear extended talk on subjects you love - The Comedians Comedian Podcast with Stuart Goldsmith being one of the best comedy podcasts I've found. I learned a lot about crowd work from the Dara O'Briain episode just before I started MC'ing gigs. It really helped and it was free!

Youtube is obviously another good source of inspiration and reference. But there's something incredible about meeting up with a group of local comedians and sharing ideas face to face. Which brings me nicely to...

Chapter Seven:
Finding Support

The right support is crucial in comedy. While there's much exhilarating fun, it can also be demoralising at times. Here's how to find the right support from the beginning of your career:

Go to writing groups

Fellow comedy writers can help fix material you didn't see working and find the punchline you've been looking for. I've experienced the impact of working with more experienced comedians first hand. Their fresh ears have helped pinpoint what was missing from bits of my material, allowing me a new perspective on my jokes.

Network locally

Comedy can be a lonely game at times. Late nights and solitary journeys. As such, try and find local like minded legends who are doing comedy and book gigs together. Car share to gigs and have a whole heap of fun, or just visit lots of service stations at weird times. Having a travel buddy who understands the comedian's life could just make you feel better about why you got home from Nottingham at 3am.

Either way, having a group of connections you can call on is helpful. As you start gigging further afield, this network of like-minded people to call on will expand across the country.

You can also get one another gigs, meaning you'll do more gigs if you buddy up as well.

Make the most of having connections in the industry. Be honest with feedback. It's not conducive to getting better at your craft if you tell each other you're great all the time and don't honestly feedback to help improve each other.

Join a comedy theatre / improv group

One of the best things I did when starting out in comedy was join an improvised comedy group.

While it's not the same as doing stand-up, comedy is comedy. Playing through improv performance allows you to learn what makes people laugh, and is the perfect place to find other comedy chums - always a good thing.

Improv definitely made me a more comfortable performer too. A quicker thinker and a better human being. It's also great fun and there's a real togetherness in the spontaneity of improv. It's a supportive experience. With one of the foundations of improv being: to have one another's backs. A way of conducting yourself I think should carry through all forms of comedy - find out how in the next chapter.

Chapter Eight:
How To Conduct Yourself

Now most acts are good well-behaved humans... But some people in comedy overlook being a decent person. I'm not sure why that is (life, I guess) but here are a few pointers on how to not look like you have no idea what you're doing in comedy (or life) when you start out:

- **Do** arrive on time.
- **Do** stay to the end if you can, the headliner will hopefully be great and you will learn from watching.
- **Do** apologise to other acts if you must leave.
- **Do** shake hands with the MC when you go on stage and after you're finished.
- **Do** thank the audience.
- **Don't** slag off other acts, either on or off stage.
- **Don't** storm out of your competition heat if you know you did terribly and won't win (I can't name names, see above).
- **Don't** get drunk and go on - I personally never drink pre-gig - it heightens confidence but lowers performance.
- **Don't** go to or perform at bringer gigs - a gig that only let people perform if they bring an audience member and stay to watch the whole show.

This is "pay to play" by proxy. It means a promoter can run a night without advertising, but the audience are there often begrudgingly and uninterested. It is a garbage format that should be avoided at all costs. (This is just my opinion and hey guys who run bringer gigs may be going "well I don't think you can teach comedy" but I am right, and they are wrong.)

Chapter Nine: Go Forth And Comedy

It's coming to the end of our time together now (crowd awws). I hope this has helped you learn a bit about comedy. Hopefully just enough to peak your interest and give you the confidence to start performing stand-up comedy in a town near you.

I personally didn't do it in the town I live in first, because then if I'd hated it I could never speak of it again.

I'm glad to say I love performing comedy. It is a privilege to stand in front of people and make them laugh.

There are so many things people could do with their time and yet they still choose to watch comedians who they have never heard of in pubs, cafes and abattoirs (A call-back. Russell Howard eat your heart out).

The best comedy nights are where the divide of audience and performers are removed, and there's that sense of "togetherness" again, in that moment. If you're wired like me, it's one of the best feelings in the world.

So, in summary, go and try doing comedy. You won't know how you feel until you do it.

I hope you love it and "I'll see you on the circuit". I like to say this to other comedy people when we part ways, because it feels very cool.

Now, go and get started.

Acknowledgements

Huge thanks go to:

Michael Tipper, who suggested I write a book in the first place and took the time to offer his own expertise as an author and a memory expert. I really value the conversations we've had about comedy and learning.

Dan Abrahams, who reinforced the book idea and helped me become a better performer and comedy coach by using his Gameface technique.

Tolmeia Gregory, for both the brilliant cover art and the babysitting!

Everyone who has taken part in a comedy workshop I have run.

All the friends I have met through Improv and to those who I have performed with, taught and been taught so much by.

The brilliant comedians who I have performed alongside.

All the people who have given me lifts to gigs.

All the friends who have endured me going from regular human to comedian and for how much they've been to watch the shows I've put on.

My parents, for raising me in a household that valued humour so highly.

My sons, for being funny and lovely.

Jon Richardson, when I doubt what I'm doing with my life I watch his Live at The Apollo set with his story about catching the last train back from London on a sunny Friday. I love it, it never fails to inspire me to keep doing comedy.

Jerry Corley, for his fantastic YouTube channel that teaches so much.

Robin Williams, who lit up the world and set a standard we all strive to achieve. We miss you.

About the Author

James Crawley is a stand-up comedian, comedy writer, improv performer, director, teacher and promoter based in the South West of England. As a comedy obsessive, James spent the first years of his comedy career actively swatting up on how to become the self-assured comic he quickly became. His first book **'A Confident Start in Stand-Up Comedy'** was written to share his comedy nerdery and save aspiring comedians the 20+ gigs worth of lessons, often touted as the only route to stand-up confidence.

Enjoyed this book? Here's what to do next!

- **Leave a review on Amazon** and let others know in how you've found it helpful.

- **Put it all into practice** and go nail your first stand-up comedy gig.

- **Work with James!** James Crawley is available to book as a stand-up, MC, improvised comedy performer, public speaker and comedy teacher. To find out more and get in touch visit https://jamescrawleycomedy.co.uk

- **Get social** You can follow James on Facebook at https://www.facebook.com/jamescrawleycomedy or Twitter https://www.twitter.com/jamescrawley

Printed in Great Britain
by Amazon